Sparkle

Explains

Colors in Art

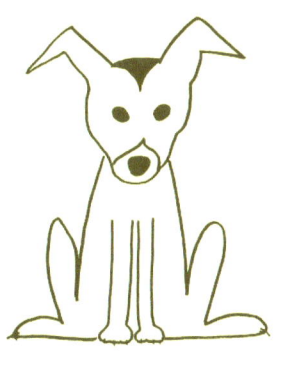

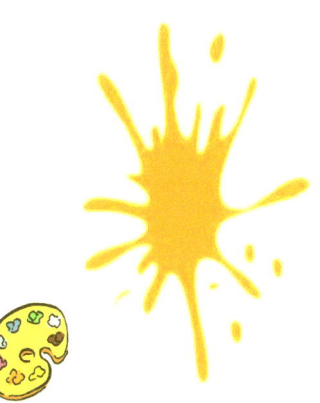

For Corley James

Thanks for teaching me the color wheel.

Hi! I'm Sparkle.

I love sparkles and bright colors. Here's what I know about colors.

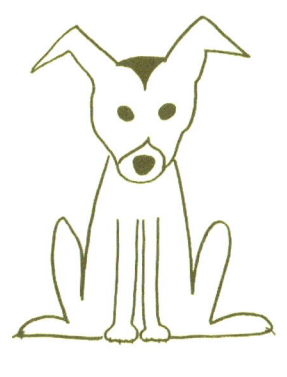

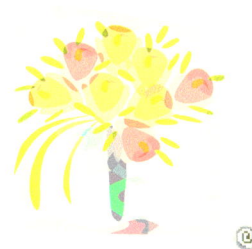

Besides black and white, artists use all of the colors of the rainbow.

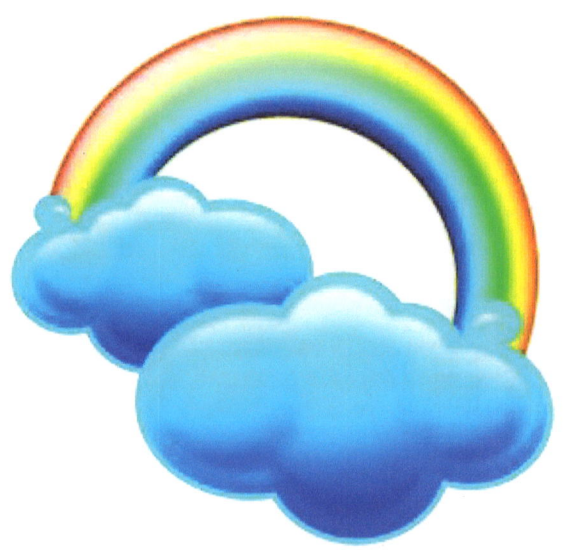

The rainbow represents the spectrum of light that eyes can see.

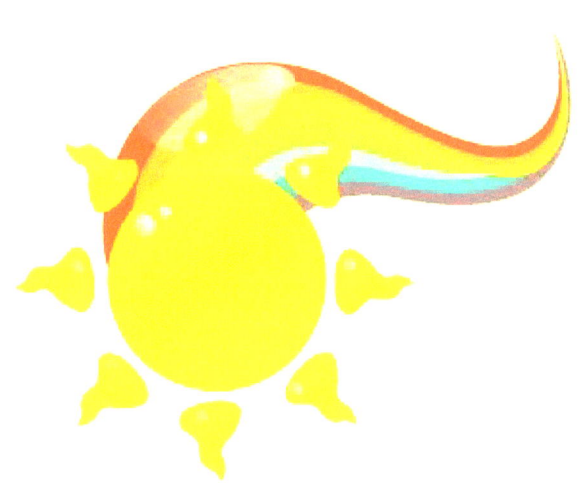

The colors of the rainbow are red, orange, yellow, green, blue, indigo and violet.

People call the colors of the rainbow Roy G. Biv. Can you guess why?

ROY G. BIV

That's right! The first letter of each of the colors spells out Roy G. Biv.

Artists can take any of the colors of the rainbow and mix them to make a new color.

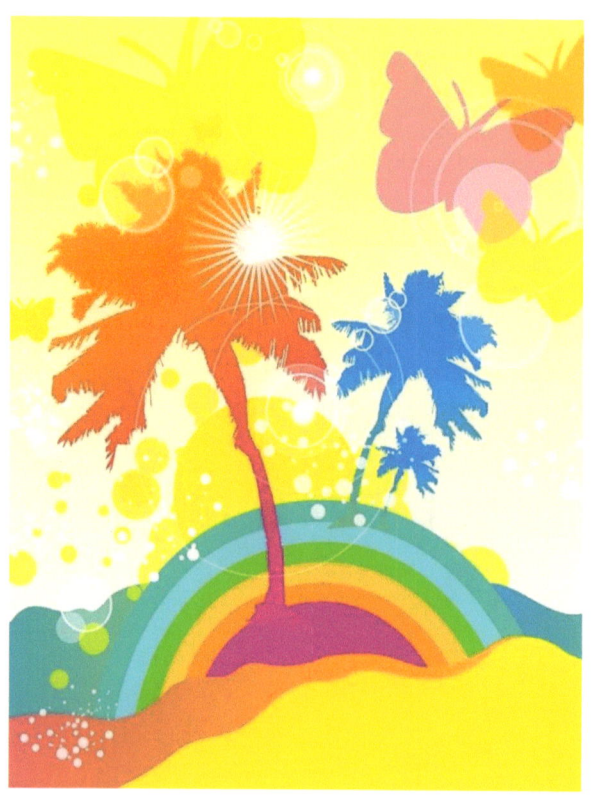

Artists start with three colors called the primary colors.

They are red, blue, and yellow.

One artist, Piet Modrian only painted with primary colors.

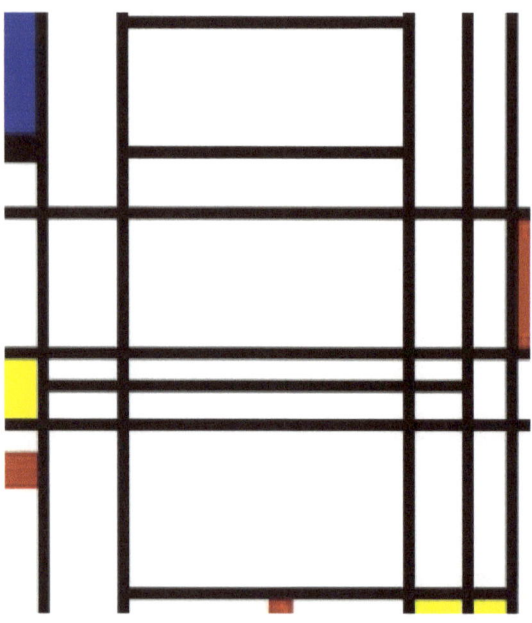

There are more than three colors. You can mix them and make secondary colors.

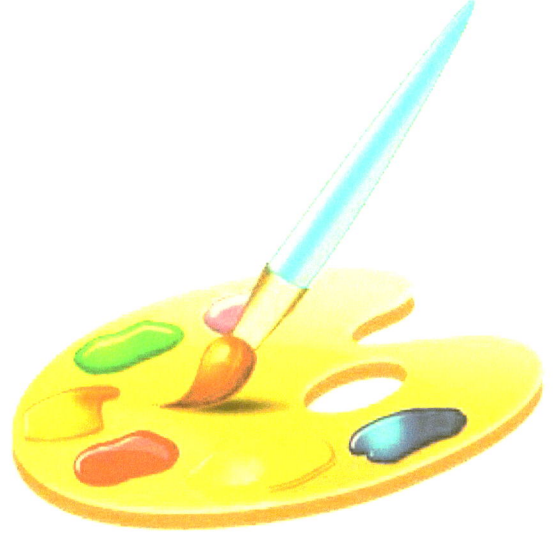

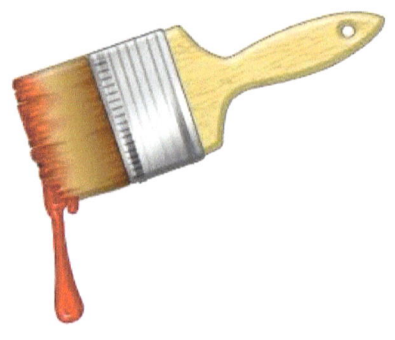

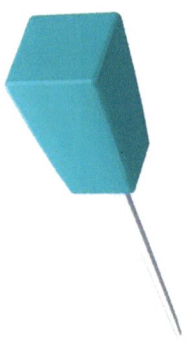

Red and blue make purple.

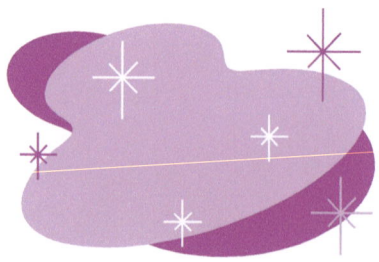

Red and yellow make
orange.

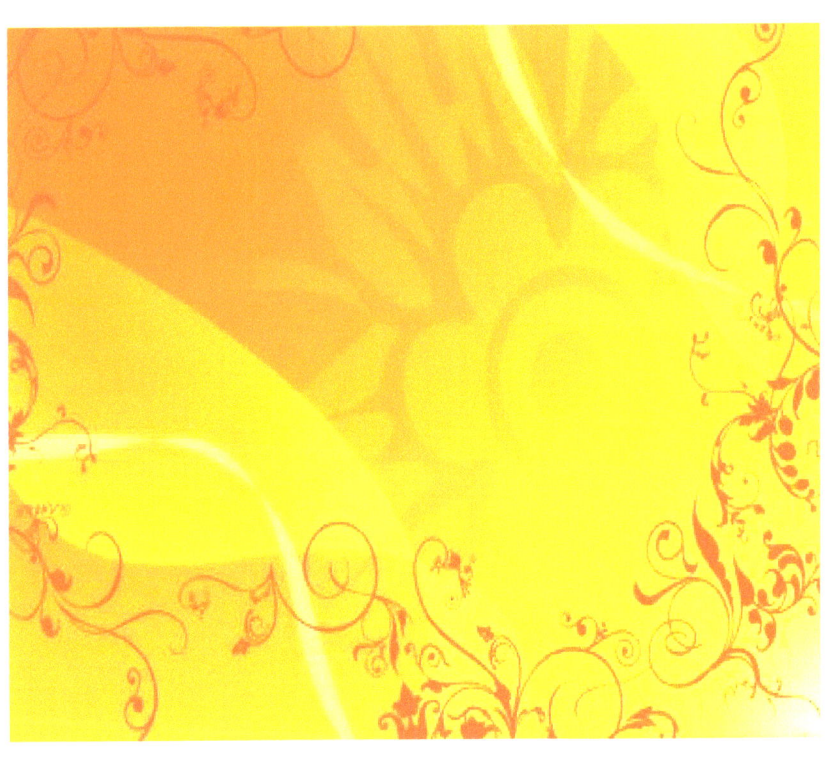

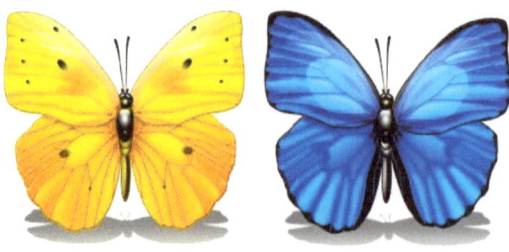

Yellow and blue make green.

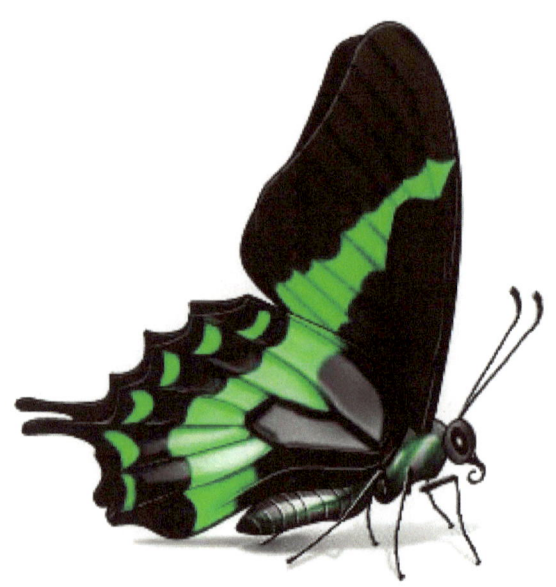

If you mix these primary colors with white, you get lighter shades.

Do you know what you get when you mix red and white?

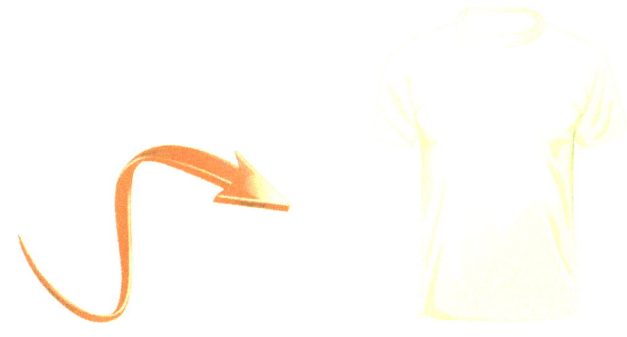

Pink! That's my favorite color.

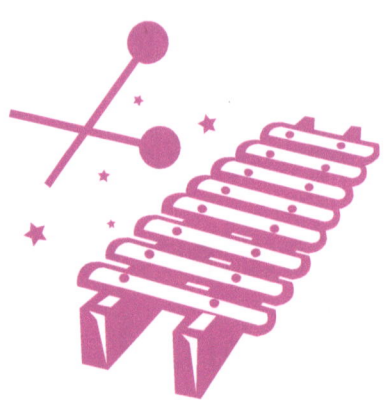

What's your favorite color?

If you don't have one, that's OK. Often, artists say they can't pick a favorite color, like Georgia O'Keefe.

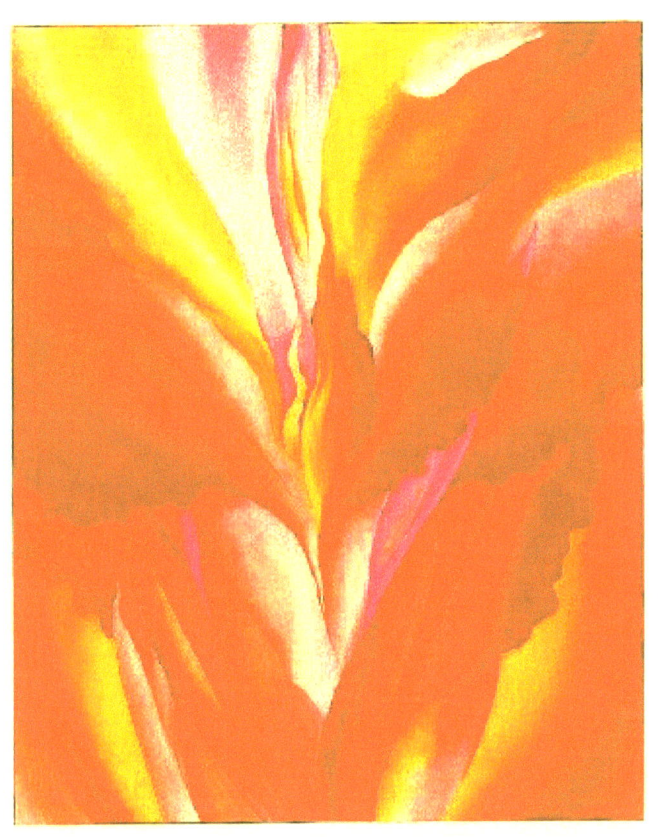

Each color has an opposite color. Look on the color wheel and find opposite colors across from each other. The opposite color is called its contrasting color.

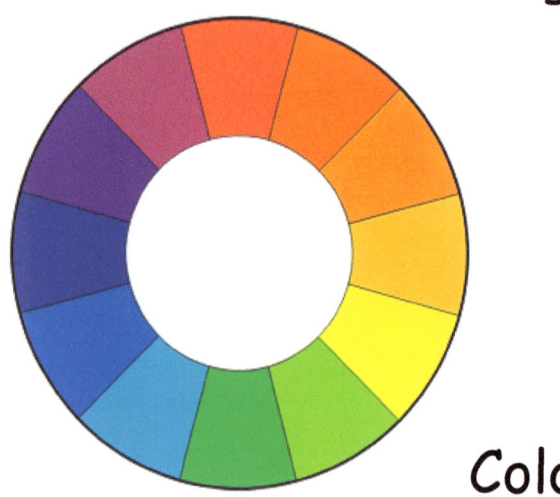

Colors similar in shades to a color are called complementary colors.

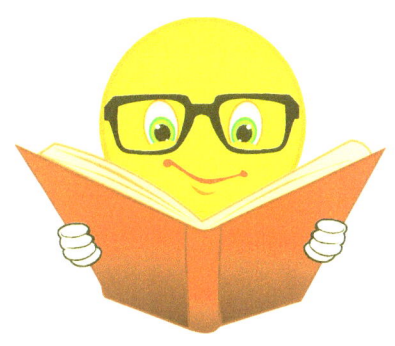

So, we learned:

primary colors

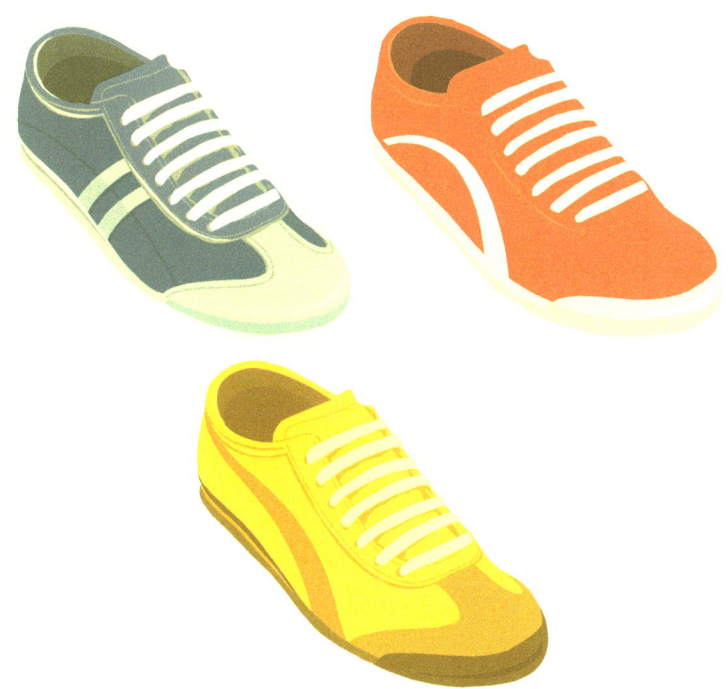

Secondary colors

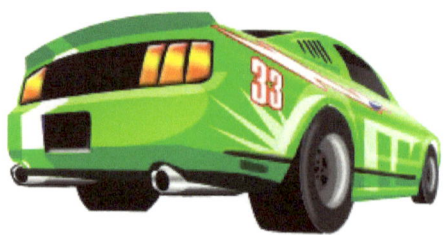

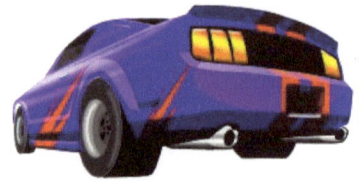

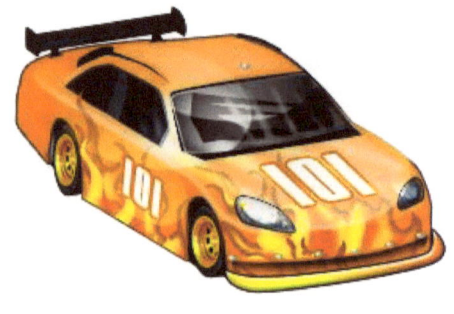

Complementary colors

That's a lot of learning about colors! Let's do a project! Now before you start any project from a drawing to making cookies with mom, get all of your supplies ready before you start.

Melting Marker Colors

You will need:

- Newspapers
- White construction paper
- Washable markers
- A paper cup of water
- Paintbrush

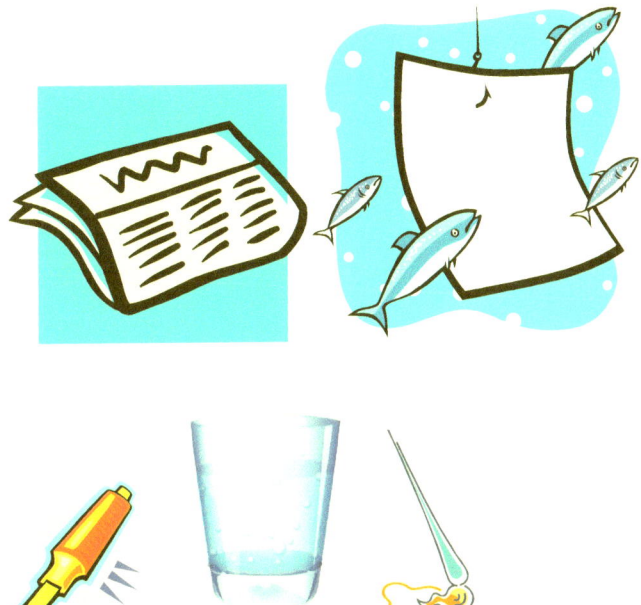

1.

Cover your craft area with newspaper. Wet a piece of heavy, light-colored paper. You're going to experiment with mixing colors. With a Paint Brush and clear water, dampen the paper.

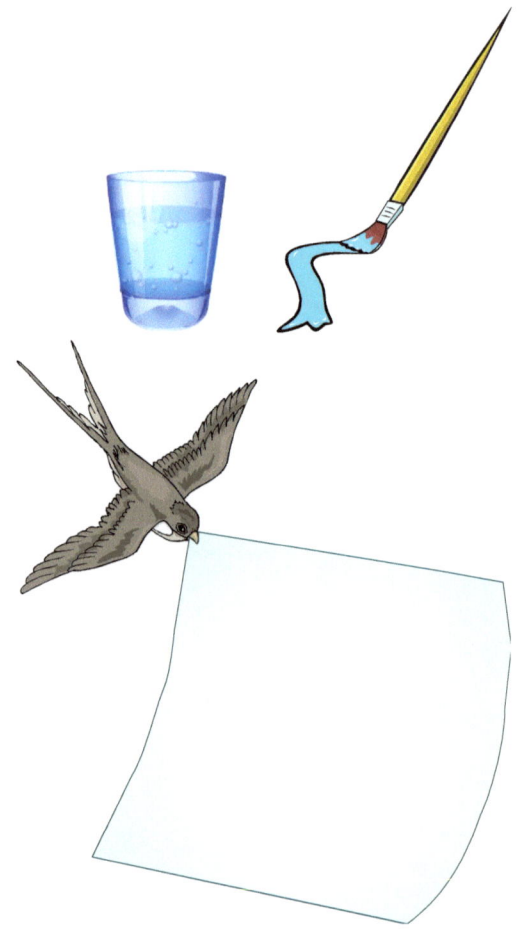

2.

Choose a Washable Marker. Make strokes of color
on your wet paper.

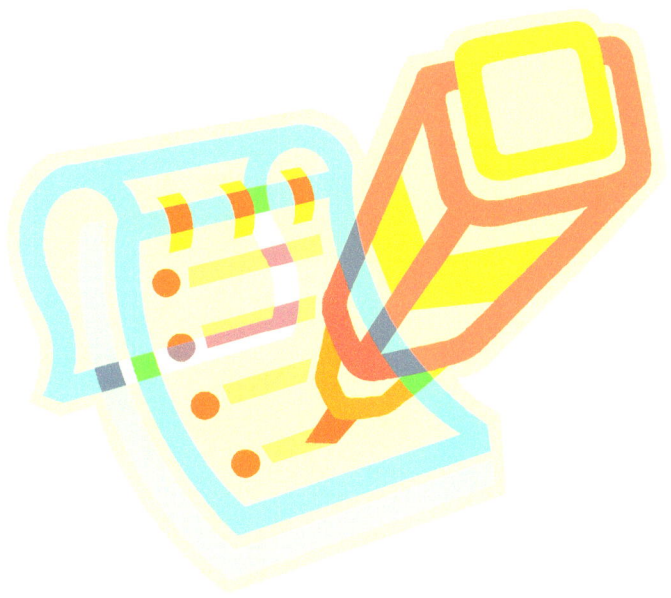

3.

Color over the first color with another color. Or put a dot or a line of one color close to another color. Watch how the colors melt into each other to create a third color, or a rainbow effect.

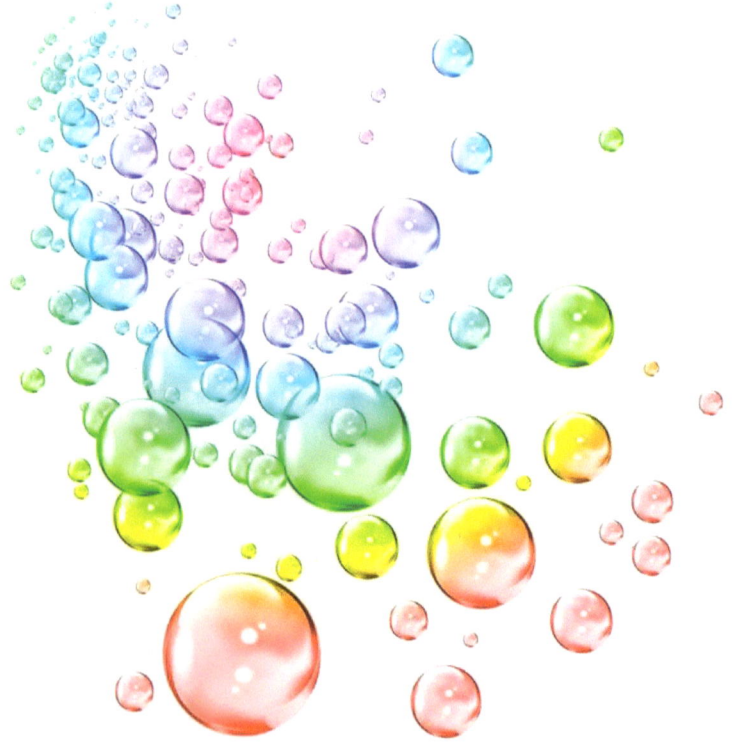

4.

Experiment with different colors and amazing effects. What new colors can you make? Air-dry your papers on more newspaper, spreading them out so they don't touch.

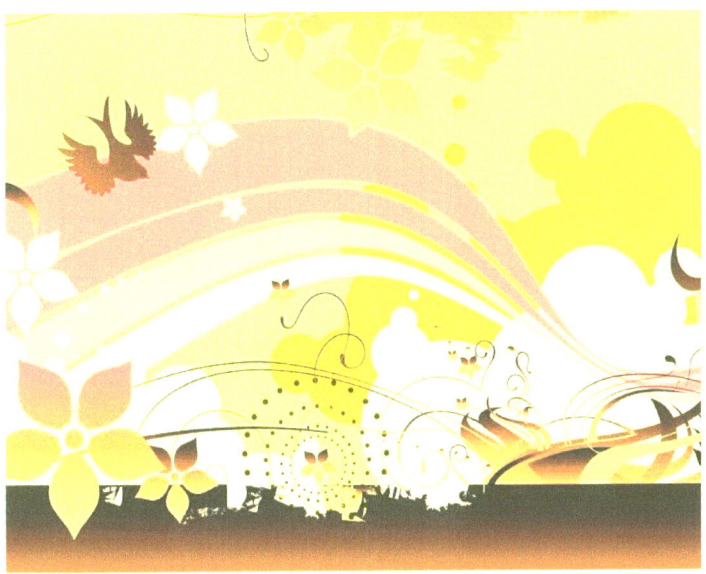

www.ingramcontent.com/pod-product-compliance
Lightning Source LLC
Chambersburg PA
CBHW041120180526
45172CB00001B/351